Blueprint to Nine Figure Legacy

Step-by-Step Strategy to Unlock the Path to a Nine Figure Legacy

Judy Theodorah

Copyright © 2024 Judy Theodorah

DEDICATION

I Dedicate this book to God Almighty for the wisdom to compile this book and make it a huge success. I also Dedicate this book to my late Mom, she is the source of my strength.

CONTENTS

Introduction

Many individuals fantasy about abandoning an enduring legacy that reaches out a long ways past their lifetime. They seek to construct a nine-figure domain that benefits themselves, yet in addition sets out open doors for a long time into the future. Not withstanding, accomplishing such a huge accomplishment requires more than living in fantasy land; It necessitates unwavering commitment, strategic planning, and an unwavering determination to achieve success.

To set out on the excursion towards a nine-figure legacy, one must initially grasp the idea of inheritance itself. Inheritance isn't characterized exclusively by material riches or assets but instead by the effect and impact a singular abandons. It includes everything from philanthropy and financial security to societal contributions and personal development. By perceiving the variety and profundity of inheritance, one acquires a more extensive viewpoint on the way that lies ahead.

At the core of opening a nine-figure heritage is a passionate longing for significance. The individual's determination to overcome obstacles, accept failure, and persistently strive for excellence is fueled by this desire. They comprehend that the way to progress is cleared with difficulties and misfortunes, however these obstacles just reinforce their purpose. They are determined to push the envelope, take calculated risks, and reject mediocrity. The key to unlocking the path to a nine-figure legacy is strategic planning. This includes making a complete guide that blueprints present moment and long haul objectives, distinguishes possible open doors and dangers, and creates procedures for expanding development. Fruitful people have a reasonable vision of their ideal inheritance and art a many-sided plan to acknowledge it. They constantly reevaluate their strategies to make sure they stay on course because they know that every decision and action they take must be in line with their ultimate goals.

A ninth-figure legacy can also be unlocked with persistence. The excursion towards massive achievement is definitely not a straight way, but instead a wild rollercoaster ride. There are snapshots of win and snapshots of misery. Be that as it may, people with a nine-figure outlook don't permit brief difficulties to dissuade them. They gain from their errors, adjust their methodology, and drive forward even with difficulty. They comprehend that each mishap is a chance for development and a venturing stone towards extreme achievement.

Additionally, philanthropy is an important factor in opening the door to a nine-figure legacy. Great people know how important it is to help others. They utilize their riches and impact to have a significant effect on the existences of others. By effectively taking part in magnanimous drives, they make a far reaching influence that stretches out a long ways past their own lifetime. Through magnanimity, they guarantee that their heritage isn't just set apart by monetary achievement yet in addition by sure change on the planet.

All in all, opening the way to a nine-figure heritage requires a remarkable blend of desire, vital preparation, determination, and charity. It's anything but an excursion for the timid, as it requests immovable devotion and an enduring obligation to self-awareness and cultural effect. However, those who are willing to embark on this extraordinary adventure will not only leave behind a lasting legacy, but they will also inspire subsequent generations to dream big and dare to accomplish the unimaginable.

PART 1: THE GROUNDWORK OF ABUNDANCE

1 Grasping the attitude of a mogul

The psychology behind their success, It is essential to first comprehend the mindset of those who have achieved financial success to build wealth. Moguls frequently share comparative mental qualities that have impelled them to their abundance. We can gain valuable insights and apply them to our journey toward financial abundance by studying the mindset of millionaires.

To many individuals, turning into a tycoon appears to be an impossible dream. They take a gander at the wealthy way of life of moguls and can't help thinking about what separates them. Is it luck, a special set of skills, or connections? Although these factors may have a minor impact, the mindset of millionaires is the primary factor that sets them apart. For those who want to achieve similar financial success, it can be helpful to understand the psychology behind their success.

1. **A Growth Perspective:** One significant characteristic shared by most moguls is a development outlook. They believe that by putting in a lot of effort, persevering, and continuing their education, they can improve their skills and intelligence. This mentality permits them to see disappointment as a venturing stone to progress and embrace difficulties as any open doors for development. They won't make do with unremarkableness and continually endeavor to work on themselves and their monetary circumstances.

2. **Goal-Orientation:** Tycoons are incredibly objective-arranged people. They set clear, quantifiable, and feasible objectives for them and guide out a way to their ideal result. They recognize that building wealth takes time, so they break their objectives down into smaller, more manageable milestones to stay focused and motivated. They maintain their progress and, in the end, achieve financial success by reviewing and revising their objectives regularly.

3: **Inconceivably curious:** One of my most important lessons for people who want to work in business is the need to know more and the desire to keep learning. I'm eager to expand my horizons, learn new things, and try new things! These qualities are needed to start and run a business because industries are always changing, and your strategy must change with them.

4: **They admit their errors:** The mindset of a millionaire transcends financial success; It includes a set of beliefs, attitudes, and actions that make successful people stand out. The capacity to take responsibility for one's errors is an essential part of this mindset. Tycoons comprehend that mix-ups are an inescapable piece of the excursion to progress, and they view them as important learning valuable open doors as opposed to disappointments.

Claiming one's slip-ups is a key characteristic of the mogul's outlook. Rather than redirecting fault or rationalizing, those with a mogul outlook get a sense of ownership of their activities and choices. They are aware that learning from their mistakes can lead to personal development and improved performance in the future.

5: **They don't put stock in karma:** Karma is a conviction begat by lethargic individuals! If you don't win the lottery, it's total nonsense. Systemic success exists. It's a result of thorough preparation, association, and readiness - NOT possibility. If you're beginning in business, do you genuinely accept karma assists you with getting financing, an extraordinary arrangement on assembling, and clients? By no means! A poop-hot plan of action, smart promoting, and tirelessness is the explanation. There is an explanation for the articulation that 'you make your karma' exists! There is nothing free or "by chance" in this world; individuals decide what they want, and only they can make it happen.

6: **They are patient and steadfast:** Achievement doesn't come about more or less by accident. It is a lengthy and frustrating process that can take years or even decades to complete. We've all heard the articulation, 'ascending the stepping stool', yet it truly is the ideal similitude to depict an excursion to progress. You'll get closer to the top with each step, but you'll need patience and balance to get there safely.

There's a typical confusion that beginning a business is an easy money scam. Sorry to break the news to you, but that is not true at all. In most cases, you will initially actually lose money. You will do whatever it takes to get there if you are persistent and motivated to succeed. If you stick with it, you'll spend your weekends conducting market research, give up social events for self-improvement.

2 Destroying restricting convictions and making engaging ones

Restricting convictions are the imperceptible obstructions that keep us from arriving at our maximum capacity. They are the profoundly imbued negative considerations, suppositions, and convictions we hold about ourselves, others, and our general surroundings. We are unable to achieve success and pursue our dreams because of these beliefs, which act as self-imposed restrictions. Notwithstanding, by recognizing and wrecking these restricting convictions, we can make engaging ones that empower us to open our actual potential and carry on with a satisfying life.

Perceiving Restricting Convictions: The most important move towards obliterating restricting convictions is to bring issues to light and distinguish them. These convictions are in many cases established in bad encounters, cultural assumptions, or youth molding. They manifest as regrettable self-talk, for example, "I'm not sufficient," "I can't make it happen," or "I will continuously fizzle." It is essential to recognize and acknowledge these beliefs to effect long-term change.

Testing Restricting Convictions: When recognized, now is the right time to challenge the legitimacy of these restricting convictions. Ask yourself: " What proof do I have to back up my belief?" Are there any elective viewpoints?" Challenge the negative suspicions and supplant them with seriously enabling and sensible ones. Rethink negative self-talk into positive attestations, moving from "I can't" to "I can" and "I will."

Looking for Proof to Help Engaging Convictions: To set the progress from restricting to engaging convictions, look for proof that upholds your new attitude. Accumulate instances of times when you have succeeded, or conquered snags. Keep in mind these accomplishments and choose to concentrate on your capabilities and strengths. Be surrounded by positive people and role models who inspire you in the same way.

Ceaseless Self-Reflection and Development: It takes time to develop beliefs that are empowering. It requires steady self-reflection and the readiness to challenge and reshape your point of view at whatever point vital. Adopt a growth mindset and view setbacks and failures as opportunities for growth. Be self-aware and receptive to new opportunities.

Accepting New Perspectives: As you keep on obliterating restricting convictions and supplanting them with engaging ones, you will start to see the world according to another viewpoint. Accept the idea that you can achieve happiness, abundance, and success. Take calculated risks and let go of the fear of failing. Be surrounded by people who share your values and motivate you to reach new heights.

Making a move and Building Certainty: Making engaging convictions is just the start; we should likewise make a move and fabricate trust in ourselves and our capacities. Separate your objectives into little, sensible advances and praise every accomplishment en route. Each step taken builds up the conviction that you are able and meriting achievement. Your confidence grows as you accomplish more, and so does your capacity to overcome any remaining limiting beliefs. Overcoming limiting beliefs is a transformative process that can lead to a life full of passion, success, and purpose. By testing and supplanting negative self-talk with engaging convictions, you open your actual potential and free yourself from self-inflicted limits. Keep in mind, that change begins from the inside, and with sincerity and determination, you can make an outlook that enables you to accomplish anything you put your energy into. In this way, embrace the cycle, have confidence in yourself, and step into a universe of boundless potential outcomes.

3 The influence of representation and sign in abundance creation

The influence of representation and signs in making abundance is a generally perceived peculiarity that has been embraced by effective people across different fields. By tackling the standards of representation and indication, people can take advantage of their psyche brain to adjust their considerations, convictions, and activities with their monetary objectives, eventually drawing overflow and success into their lives.

Representation includes making mental pictures of one's ideal results and encounters. When applied to abundance creation, people picture themselves making monetary progress, carrying on with an existence of overflow, and understanding their financial objectives. By distinctively envisioning these situations and encounters, they can program their psyche brain to pursue these goals, in this way upgrading their concentration and inspiration towards abundance creation.

Related to representation, the act of sign includes intentionally guiding one's contemplations and energy towards the achievement of riches and overflow. This includes keeping a positive outlook, adjusting one's contemplations and convictions to the conviction that abundance is feasible, and reliably confirming and imagining one's monetary achievement. ,

The force of sign stretches out past simple positive reasoning; it includes making a propelled move towards one's monetary goals. By setting clear expectations, making a game plan, and reliably pursuing their objectives, people can show riches and overflow in their lives. In addition, the general pattern of good following good, which sets that like draws in like, is intently attached to the standards of representation and appearance. By keeping a positive and bountiful outlook, people are accepted to draw in comparative energy and potentially open doors into their lives, in this manner making the way for dramatic abundance creation and monetary achievement.

It's vital to take note that while representation and sign are amazing assets in abundance creation, they should be joined by tenacious exertion, steadiness, and a readiness to proceed with well-balanced plans of action. The course of representation and sign fills in as an impetus for enabling people to have faith in their true capacity for monetary achievement and to make a propelled move towards accomplishing their objectives. , The influence of perception and sign in abundance creation lies in its capacity to adjust one's considerations, convictions, and activities with their monetary objectives, subsequently drawing in overflow and thriving into their lives. By saddling these practices, people can open their maximum capacity for monetary achievement and make a pathway towards the existence of riches and overflow.

4 Embracing difficulties and misfortunes as any open doors for development

"In each trouble lies a chance for development," said the popular physicist Albert Einstein. This significant assertion stresses the significance of fostering a development mentality, which can essentially have an impact on how we view and move toward difficulties and misfortunes in our lives. By embracing these impediments as any open doors for individual and expert development, we can open our maximum capacity and make more prominent progress.

At the point when we discuss a development outlook, we allude to the conviction that our capacities and knowledge can be created through commitment, exertion, and constancy. Rather than being restricted by a decent mentality that expects our characteristics to be intrinsic and unchangeable, a development outlook empowers us to embrace difficulties and mishaps as venturing stones toward progress.

Challenges are a characteristic piece of life. Whether it's confronting a troublesome undertaking at work, managing individual mishaps, or experiencing deterrents on the way to accomplishing our objectives, embracing these difficulties with a development mentality is fundamental. Rather than staying away from them or feeling crushed, we can utilize these hindrances for our potential benefit.

One method for moving toward difficulties is by reexamining them as any open doors for learning and development. Instead of reviewing them as barricades, we can take on a positive outlook and consider them to be opportunities to extend our insight, obtain new abilities, and upgrade our critical abilities to think. Embracing difficulties as any open doors assists us with creating flexibility, assurance, and versatility, which are crucial resources for long-haul achievement.

Difficulties are another region where a development mentality can assume a critical part. Misfortunes can be disheartening and make us question our capacities. In any case, a development mentality permits us to consider misfortunes to be impermanent difficulties, not super-durable disappointments. By zeroing in on the examples gained from these mishaps, we can foster a more prominent comprehension of ourselves, our assets, and our shortcomings. This self-reflection enables us to make vital changes, work on our procedures, and return more grounded than at any other time.

One compelling methodology for embracing difficulties and misfortunes is to foster a development-situated self-talk. Rather than participating in bad self-talk that supports restrictions and self-questioning, we ought to help ourselves to remember the development expected in each tough spot. By supplanting considerations like "I can't do this" with "I haven't dominated this yet, yet with exertion and devotion, I will improve," we shift our outlook and free ourselves up to development and advancement.

Embracing difficulties and misfortunes as any open doors for development likewise requires a change in our disposition towards disappointment. Rather than review disappointment as a conclusive endpoint, we ought to remember it as a venturing stone toward progress. Disappointments offer significant illustrations and bits of knowledge that can direct our future endeavors. By embracing disappointment as a characteristic piece of the growing experience, we become more open to facing challenges, exploring different avenues regarding new methodologies, and eventually making more prominent progress.

Understanding the attitude of tycoons is fundamental for creating financial momentum. By perceiving the mental attributes that add to their prosperity, like fearlessness, assurance, and a development outlook, we can support these characteristics inside ourselves. Also, by wrecking restricting convictions, embracing representation and indication methods, and surveying difficulties as any open doors for development, we establish the groundwork for accomplishing enduring riches and monetary overflow.

PART 2: BUILDING A SOLID FINANCIAL PLAN

5 learning to set goals effectively

Financial goal setting that is both ambitious and doable is a crucial skill that can make a big difference in a person's success and overall financial well-being. In this regard, mastering the art of goal setting necessitates effective planning, strategic thinking, and determination. People's ability to set and achieve ambitious financial goals can be enhanced by adhering to a few key principles and employing specific strategies.

1. Foster an Unmistakable Vision: The most vital move towards setting aggressive monetary targets is to foster an unmistakable vision of what you need to accomplish. Envision your objectives and figure out the degree of their aspiration. For instance, if you want to save a certain amount of money, figure out why you want to save it, such as to put down a down payment on a house, start a business, or retire early. This clearness will fuel your inspiration and assist you with keeping on track all through your excursion.

2. **Set goals that are specific and measurable:** When setting financial goals, it's critical to be specific and measurable. Rather than enigmatically expecting to "set aside more cash," be exact about the sum you need to save and the course of events you wish to accomplish. Explicit objectives consider better preparation and following advancement, while quantifiable objectives empower you to precisely survey your accomplishments.

3. **Embrace the Watchful Plan**: In goal setting, utilizing the Splendid framework can be useful. Addresses that are unambiguous, quantifiable, feasible, appropriate, and time-bound are smart. Survey your cash-

related fixations as opposed to these rules, guaranteeing everyone lines up with the Smart standards. This structure assists with refining targets, makes them more reachable, and gives a manual for progress.

4. **Divide your goals into more manageable milestones:** Aggressive monetary targets can be overpowering, particularly when seen as a solitary, huge goal. Separating them into more modest achievements makes them more reasonable and considers ordinary advancement appraisal. You can focus on each milestone individually and celebrate victories along the way by breaking up a large goal into smaller parts, which boosts motivation and confidence.

5. **Focus on and Spotlight on Your Objectives:** It is critical to focus on your monetary objectives and abstain from getting diverted by other enticing open doors or costs. Identify the most important objectives and commit the necessary resources and time to achieving them. By remaining fixed on your first concerns, you increase your possibilities of accomplishing them within your ideal period.

6. **Make a Sensible Monetary Arrangement:** To achieve ambitious financial goals, a realistic financial plan is essential. It involves looking at your current financial situation, figuring out where you get your money, keeping track of your expenses, and figuring out where you can spend less or spend more effectively. A very much-created plan will act as a guide, assisting you with settling on suitable monetary choices and guaranteeing you designate adequate assets towards accomplishing your objectives.

7. **Consistently Survey and Change Objectives:** As life advances, conditions and needs might change. In this way, it is urgent to audit and change your monetary objectives routinely. Direct occasional evaluations to guarantee the objectives you set to line up with your desires and current circumstances. On the off chance that fundamental, make acclimations to your objectives, timetables, or even the objective add up to keep up with their aspiration while holding their feasibility.

8. **Keep a positive attitude and practice discipline:** Excelling an objective setting requires a positive mentality and trained activity. Monetary excursions can be testing, and difficulties or allurements might emerge en route. Develop an uplifting perspective, embrace difficulties as learning potential open doors, and stay trained in your ways of managing money and reserve funds techniques. Keep in mind, that accomplishing aggressive monetary objectives is a long-distance race, not a run.

9. **Look for Direction and Responsibility:** Your progress toward

achieving your financial goals can be significantly aided by seeking direction and accountability. Consider counseling a monetary consultant or tutor who can offer bits of knowledge, master guidance, and assist with keeping you responsible all through your excursion. Imparting your objectives to a believed companion or relative can likewise give an additional layer of help and consolation.

10. **Recognize accomplishments:** Praising accomplishments, regardless of how little, is fundamental for staying inspired and keeping up with energy. Perceive and compensate yourself at whatever point you achieve an achievement or accomplish a monetary objective. Treating yourself to something you like is one way to celebrate, as is reflecting on your accomplishments and appreciating your progress.

It takes practice, dedication, and perseverance to master the art of setting financial goals that are both ambitious and attainable. By applying these standards and procedures reliably, you can further develop your objective-setting abilities, upgrade your monetary advancement, and eventually accomplish the monetary achievement you strive for. Keep in mind, that each step in the right direction towards your monetary objectives carries you more like a solid and prosperous future.

6 Developing an extensive financial plan

Making an extensive monetary guide is fundamental for accomplishing long-haul monetary strength and achievement. It includes three key parts: investing, saving, and making a budget. You will be able to effectively manage your money, accumulate wealth, and ensure a brighter future if you incorporate these practices into your financial plan.

1. **Budgeting:** Planning is essential to any monetary arrangement. It entails keeping track of your income and expenses and allocating your funds following your financial objectives. Here are the moves toward making a viable financial plan:

a) Evaluate your pay: Determine your total income from investments, side jobs, bonuses, salaries, and other sources.

b) Track costs: Spending on things like housing, utilities, transportation, groceries, entertainment, and paying off debt can help you keep an eye on your spending. This recognizes regions where you can scale back and save.

c) Put forth monetary objectives: Set both short-term and long-term financial objectives, such as retiring, paying off debt, saving for unexpected expenses, or buying a house. Relegate explicit sums and cutoff times to every objective to keep yourself responsible.

d) Distribute funds: Make a budget that prioritizes essential expenses, savings, paying off debt, and discretionary spending. Put your financial objectives first by allocating a significant portion of your income to saving money and paying off debt.

e) Audit and change: Consistently audit your financial plan and make changes on a case-by-case basis. This guarantees that your financial plan stays significant and versatile to changes in your pay or costs.

2. **Saving:** Building financial security and achieving financial objectives in the future require saving. You can save more money by using these

strategies:

a) Fund for emergencies: Put money aside for unforeseen circumstances like a medical emergency, a job loss, or home repairs. Put three to six months' worth of living expenses in an account that is liquid and simple to access.

b) Momentary objectives: Save for transient objectives like excursions, vehicle acquisitions, or home redesigns. Set up automatic transfers to a separate account specifically designated for these objectives after determining the required sum.

c) Savings for retirement: Contribute consistently to retirement records, for example, individual retirement accounts (IRAs), or benefits plans. Exploit business matching commitments if accessible.

d) Streamline savings: To guarantee consistent savings growth, set up automatic transfers from your income to various savings accounts. Treat investment funds as a non-debatable cost.

e) Decrease pointless costs: Examine your spending patterns to find areas where you can save money. Put the money you saved toward your savings objectives.

3. Investing: Putting away permits your cash to develop over the long run, giving you an amazing chance to create riches and accomplish long-haul monetary objectives. When developing an investment plan, take the following into consideration:

a) Hazard resistance: By understanding your willingness and capacity to tolerate fluctuations in investment returns, you can determine your risk tolerance. This will assist with deciding the proper blend of ventures for your portfolio.

b) Multiplication: Spread your speculations across various resource classes (stocks, bonds, land, and so on.) to lower the risk. Enhancement helps smooth out expected misfortunes and improves the probability of positive returns.

c) Time skyline: Take into consideration your investment time horizon, which is the amount of time before you need the money you've invested. Investing strategies can be more aggressive with longer time horizons.

d) Seek advice from professionals: Consult a financial advisor if you're unsure about investing or want personalized advice. They can help you navigate investment options and create a plan that fits your needs.

e) Keep an eye on and rebalance: Routinely survey your speculation portfolio to guarantee it lines up with your objectives. Maintain the desired asset allocation and adjust for changing market conditions by rebalancing regularly.

Keep in mind that putting together a comprehensive financial roadmap necessitates persistence, discipline, and patience. Carrying out these practices won't just assist you with successfully dealing with your cash yet in addition make you ready for long haul monetary security, abundance creation, and a satisfying monetary future.

7 How to bring in your cash to work for you

Using influence keenly is a strong procedure that can assist you with bringing in your cash work for you. Influence includes utilizing acquired reserves or monetary instruments to expand your expected profits from speculation. When applied accurately, it can speed up abundance creation and open up doors that may somehow or another be far off. Notwithstanding, it's fundamental to approach influence with alertness and comprehend how to explore its expected dangers. Here is a thorough manual for using influence brilliantly:

1. **Figure out the idea of influence:** Influence empowers you to control a bigger measure of resources or ventures with a more modest starting speculation. It permits you to intensify your likely gains yet in addition opens you to a more serious gamble. It's critical to have a reasonable comprehension of how influence functions and its likely ramifications.

2. **Use influence for money-producing resources:** One compelling method for utilizing shrewdly is by utilizing it to obtain pay creating resources like land or organizations. By utilizing a piece of the price tag through a home loan or business credit, you can utilize the rental pay or benefits produced by the resource to cover the credit installments. This permits you to develop value and create recurring, automated revenue without utilizing the entirety of your capital.

3. **Assess the gamble reward proportion:** Before utilizing influence, cautiously evaluate the gamble reward proportion of the speculation opportunity. Consider the possible returns, the dependability of the speculation, economic situations, and the potential disadvantage chances. Guarantee that the expected returns offset the dangers implied.

4. **Further develop reliability:** To get to good use choices, center around

working on your financial soundness. Keep a decent rating by making convenient installments, overseeing obligations capably, and staying away from unnecessary getting. A solid credit profile expands your capacity to protect credits with positive terms.

5. **Broaden your speculations**: Enhancement is a key gamble in the board system while utilizing influence. Spread your speculations across different resource classes and markets to moderate the effect of any single venture turning sour. This shields your portfolio from critical misfortunes in the event that a specific venture doesn't proceed true to form.

6. **Have an emergency course of action**: Think about the potential most pessimistic scenario situations and have an emergency course of action set up. This could include saving store reserves or having elective kinds of revenue to cover any startling difficulties. Being ready for unexpected conditions can assist you with exploring likely difficulties and limiting their effect.

7. **Limit your influence proportion**: Keep a moderate influence proportion to decrease the gamble of overstretching yourself monetarily. Keep away from inordinate getting and hold back nothing where you can easily deal with the obligation reimbursements in any event, during times of financial vulnerability. This gives a security net and guarantees that you don't turn out to be excessively dependent on influence.

8. **Consistent checking and change**: Routinely screen your utilized ventures and change your methodology depending on the situation. Remain refreshed on market patterns, loan fees, and changes in the venture scene. Be ready to make fundamental acclimations to your influence position to upgrade returns and oversee gambles.

9. **Look for proficient exhortation:** In the event that you're new to utilizing or have a questionable outlook on specific venture open doors, think about looking for direction from a monetary consultant or expert with experience in utilizing systems. They can give master experiences, assess what is going on, and assist you with settling on informed choices.

10. **Study and learn**: Influence is a complex monetary idea, and it's essential to teach yourself about its subtleties persistently. Understand books, go to workshops, follow trustworthy monetary sources, and take part in conversations with experienced financial backers to develop how you might interpret influence and how it very well may be used shrewdly.

Keep in mind, using influence wisely requires cautious thought, research, and a restrained methodology. By understanding the dangers implied, enhancing your ventures, and remaining informed, you can amplify the possible advantages while limiting the drawbacks. Using influence keenly can be an incredible asset to bring in your cash work for yourself and speed up your way to monetary achievement.

8 The significance of diverse sources of revenue

Enhancing revenue streams is a urgent methodology that can give monetary security, dependability, and potential open doors for development. Depending on a solitary type of revenue can leave you helpless against startling monetary slumps, industry-explicit difficulties, or individual mishaps. By developing different income streams, you can spread risk, improve your procuring potential, and make a stronger monetary establishment. Here is an exhaustive manual for the significance of differentiating revenue sources:

1. **Upgrading Monetary Security:** Depending entirely on a solitary work or business for money leaves you powerless against the vulnerabilities of the gig market or industry-explicit disturbances. Enhancing your revenue streams extends to security against unanticipated conditions like employment opportunity misfortune, monetary downturns, or changes in market interest. Having various wellsprings of income makes a security net, decreasing the effect of any single revenue stream being upset.

2. **Boosting Procuring Potential**: By expanding your pay, you can take advantage of different chances to augment your acquiring potential. This could include chasing after independent work, putting resources into land, making and selling computerized items, or beginning a side business. Each extra stream of pay can possibly add to your general monetary prosperity, prompting expanded procuring power and more noteworthy monetary adaptability.

3. **Flexibility in Changing Financial Circumstances**: Monetary variances can fundamentally affect explicit enterprises or areas. By expanding revenue streams across various ventures or resource classes,

you can relieve the effect of financial slumps. For instance, if one industry encounters a decay, other enhanced revenue streams might keep on performing great, giving soundness during testing times.

4. **Setting out Automated revenue Open doors:** Differentiating revenue streams permits you to investigate recurring, automated revenue open doors. This could remember financial planning for stocks, securities, or land properties that produce progressing pay with insignificant dynamic contribution. Automated sources of income can give long haul monetary dependability and the adaptability to seek after private interests and interests.

5. **Opening Ways to New Open Doors:** Having different revenue streams can set out open doors to investigate new pursuits, projects, and pioneering pursuits. It gives the opportunity to go ahead with carefully thought-out plans of action, seek after meaningful ventures, or put resources into regions that line up with your inclinations and abilities. Enhancing revenue streams can prompt a more extravagant and satisfying proficient and individual life.

6. **Decreasing Reliance on a Solitary Source:** Depending exclusively on one boss or business for money can make a reliance that restricts your opportunity and adaptability. By enhancing revenue sources, you decrease the dependence on any single wellspring of income and oversee your monetary predetermination. This can prompt expanded certainty and a feeling of strengthening in dealing with your funds.

7. **Adaptability and Flexibility**: Developing various revenue streams upgrades your versatility to changing conditions and advancing business sector elements. It permits you to turn and change your pay technique in view of arising amazing open doors or changes in customer conduct. With assorted revenue sources, you can explore changes in the monetary scene all the more successfully.

8. **Chasing after Private and Expert Development:** Expanding revenue streams supports consistent learning, ability advancement, and self-improvement. It might include obtaining new abilities, organizing with assorted gatherings of experts, or investigating various ventures. This consistent advancement can prompt a more unique and improving profession and self-awareness.

9. **Long haul Establishing financial stability:** Broadening of revenue streams adds to long haul establishing long term financial stability. By decisively distributing pay from different sources, you can assign assets towards speculations, investment funds, and retirement arranging. This approach can lay the preparation for monetary freedom and a safe

future.

Expanding revenue streams is a central system for accomplishing monetary strength, security, and adaptability. By chasing after different roads for creating pay, people can shield their monetary prosperity, open new open doors, and construct a strong and versatile monetary establishment. Whether through speculations, independent work, business venture, or automated revenue systems, developing different income streams is vital to a decent and reasonable monetary future.

All in all, constructing a strong monetary diagram requires a blend of objective setting, making an extensive monetary guide, utilizing shrewdly, and broadening revenue sources. By becoming amazing at objective setting, you can set reachable targets and remain spurred on your monetary excursion. Making a complete monetary guide assists you with dealing with your funds really and pursue informed choices. Using influence keenly can assist with improving your speculations, while expanding revenue streams gives monetary security and upgrades your development potential. Keep in mind, fabricating a strong monetary diagram is a long lasting cycle, and it's critical to consistently survey and change your systems as your conditions change.

PART 3: TACKLING THE FORCE OF SELF-CONTROL

9 Creating extreme concentration

Creating extreme concentration is fundamental for making progress and arriving at one's objectives. In the present high-speed and innovation-driven world, interruptions are plentiful, making it trying to keep fixed on the main thing. In any case, by executing specific systems and keeping areas of strength for your objectives, it's feasible to dispense with interruptions and foster a steady center that will move you towards progress.

To start, recognize that normal interruptions impede your concentration. These interruptions can be both outside and inner. Outer interruptions incorporate virtual entertainment, email warnings, calls, and loud conditions. Interior interruptions, then again, are contemplations and feelings that redirect your consideration from the main job. By perceiving these interruptions, you can find proactive ways to moderate their effect.

One of the best ways of wiping out interruptions is to establish a helpful and centered workplace. Find a tranquil spot where interferences are far-fetched, like a devoted office or a quiet corner in your home. Moreover, diminish visual interruptions by keeping your work area mess-free and coordinated. Use sound-blocking earphones or encompassing music to shut out foundation commotion and make a serene air that helps focus.

Advanced interruptions, particularly virtual entertainment and email, can be especially slippery. To battle them, lay out clear limits and rules for innovation utilization. Set explicit times for browsing messages and cut off virtual entertainment utilization to assigned breaks. Use efficiency applications or site blockers to briefly limit admittance to diverting sites and applications during centered work periods. By laying out these limits, you can recover command over your consideration and allot it towards your objectives.

One more critical part of creating exacting concentration is dealing with your time. Make a timetable that focuses on your most significant errands and designates explicit time blocks for centered work. By utilizing time-hindering strategies, you put away devoted periods for conscious practice, profound work, or whatever other exercises that require extraordinary focus. Setting cutoff times for errands likewise makes a need to get going, prompting uplifted concentration and efficiency.

Close by dealing with your time, it's fundamental to deal with your energy levels to keep up with the center. Enjoy normal in the middle between work meetings to re-energize and revive. Take part in exercises that advance unwinding and decrease pressure, like reflection, exercise, or investing energy in nature. Focus on getting adequate rest, as an absence of rest can extraordinarily frustrate center and mental capacities. By guaranteeing your energy levels are ideal, you can support the center for additional drawn-out periods and produce greater work.

Remaining focused on your objectives is vital for creating extreme concentration. Characterize your objectives obviously and grasp the explanations for them; this will give you a feeling of inspiration and inspiration. Record your objectives and make a visual portrayal, for example, a dream board, that helps you to remember what you're pursuing. Consistently surveying and thinking about your objectives will assist you with remaining committed and zeroed in, during testing times. Responsibility is one more pivotal component in keeping up with concentration and responsibility. Share your objectives with a confided-in companion, tutor, or mentor who can offer help and consider you responsible. Ordinary registrations and advance updates can assist with guaranteeing that you keep focused and zero in on your goals. Encircling yourself with similar people who share comparative desires can likewise give an additional layer of responsibility and backing.

Finally, developing self-control and resilience is essential. Creating careful concentration requires predictable exertion and commitment. Figure out how to express no to interruptions, both inside and outer. Push through snapshots of self-uncertainty or fatigue by helping yourself to remember the more prominent reason behind your work. Embrace disappointment as a feature of the educational experience and use difficulties as any open doors for development and improvement. By fortifying your purpose and flexibility muscles, you will be better prepared to keep fixed on your objectives despite any difficulties that might emerge.

creating careful concentration is critical for disposing of interruptions and remaining focused on your objectives. Through establishing an engaged workplace, overseeing investment, and cultivating responsibility and responsibility, you can foster the unflinching center important for making progress. Remain trained, be patient, and keep your focus on the big picture - and the careful concentration you look for will turn into an inborn piece of your day-to-day existence.

10 Procedures for upgrading efficiency

Beating stalling is a typical test that many individuals face while attempting to upgrade efficiency. Stalling can impede progress, create pointless pressure, and keep people from arriving at their maximum capacity. In any case, with the right systems and outlook, defeating dawdling and lifting productivity is conceivable. Here is a far-reaching guide to conquering dawdling and improving efficiency:

1. **Comprehend the Main drivers:** Perceive the fundamental explanations for your inclination to tarry. It very well may be dread of disappointment, compulsiveness, absence of inspiration, or feeling overpowered by the job that needs to be done. Distinguishing these main drivers can assist you with creating designated methodologies to address them.

2. **Put forth Clear Objectives and Boundaries:** Characterize your objectives and separate them into more modest, reasonable errands. This empowers you to zero in on unambiguous activities, making them not so much scary but rather more attainable. Laying out needs assists you with designating your significant investment successfully, decreasing the probability of hesitation.

3. **Make a Point-by-point Activity Plan:** Foster a definite arrangement that frames the important stages to achieve your objectives. Having a guide assists you with remaining coordinated and gives a reasonable bearing to each undertaking. Separating the work into more modest, significant advances makes it simpler to get everything rolling and keep up with force.

4. Begin Little and Gather Speed: Frequently, the hardest piece of any assignment is getting everything rolling. Defeat this underlying opposition by beginning with little, reasonable undertakings. By finishing these, you gather speed and gain certainty, making it simpler to handle additional difficult errands later on.

5. Use Time Usage Methods: Viable use of time effectively is urgent for fighting stalling. Methods like the Pomodoro Procedure (working in short overflows with ordinary breaks), time hindering (allocating explicit schedule openings to various errands), and setting cutoff times can assist you with remaining on track and utilizing your time.

6. Kill Interruptions: Recognize and wipe out or limit interruptions that add to tarrying. This could include switching off notices on your telephone, making a committed work area, or utilizing site blockers to confine admittance to diverting sites during work hours. Establishing a favorable climate liberated from interruptions improves concentration and efficiency.

7. Foster a Daily schedule: Laying out a steady normal can assist with combatting lingering by creating a feeling of construction and discipline. Set explicit times for work, breaks, and recreation exercises, and adhere to the timetable however much as could be expected. A routine decreases choice weariness and lays out useful propensities.

8. Practice Self-Empathy: Be caring to yourself while confronting tarrying. Stay away from self-analysis or negative self-talk, as these can advance demotivate and obstruct progress. All things considered, practice self-empathy by recognizing that everybody encounters difficulties and spotlight on gaining from them and making a positive move.

9. Find Responsibility Accomplices: Offer your objectives and progress to somebody who can consider you responsible. This could be a companion, relative, or coach who can offer help, consolation, and delicate suggestions to keep focused. Responsibility accomplices can assist you with conquering dawdling and remaining focused on your objectives.

10. Observe Progress and Prize Yourself: Recognize and commend your achievements en route. By remunerating yourself for getting done with responsibilities or arriving at achievements, you support a positive way of behaving and propel yourself to keep gaining ground.

11. Center around the Advantages: Help yourself to remember the advantages and rewards that come from conquering dawdling and being more useful. Imagine the feeling of achievement, decreased pressure, and expanded open doors that look for you once you overcome hesitation.

12. Practice Care and Stress Decrease: Hesitation can now and then be powered by pressure, tension, or a dispersed brain. Integrating care methods, like profound breathing activities, contemplation, or journaling, can assist with quieting the psyche, lessen feelings of anxiety, and increment concentration and lucidity.

Defeating dawdling and improving efficiency requires mindfulness, discipline, and successful techniques. By figuring out the basic reasons for lingering, executing time usage procedures, disposing of interruptions, and rehearsing self-sympathy, people can foster an engaged and useful mentality. Keep in mind, that defeating tarrying is an excursion, so show restraint toward yourself, remain committed, and commend the headway you make en route. With diligence and the right methodologies, you can beat delaying and open your actual efficiency potential.

11 Putting resources into training and self-improvement

Constant learning and putting resources into schooling and self-improvement have become fundamental in the present quickly changing and exceptionally cutthroat world. The days when we could depend entirely on our conventional training to get a steady profession and prevail in life are a distant memory. As innovation progresses, businesses develop, and new abilities arise, the need to ceaselessly learn and fill in our insight and capacities has become significant.

One of the primary reasons nonstop learning is significant is that it permits people to remain pertinent and versatile in their picked fields. Previously, individuals could hope to work for a solitary organization or in a particular industry for their whole vocation. Notwithstanding, with mechanical headways and financial movements, occupations are turning out to be more transient, and enterprises are changing at an exceptional rate. To stay cutthroat in the gig market, it is urgent to continually refresh our abilities and information to line up with the most recent industry patterns.

Besides, constant learning encourages self-improvement and advancement. It permits people to grow their points of view, investigate new areas of premium, and foster new points of view. Participating in persistent learning can prompt expanded self-assurance, as gaining new information and abilities can engage people to take on new difficulties and potentially open doors. It additionally assists people with conquering deterrents and adjusting to change, which are significant characteristics in both individual and expert life.

Putting resources into instruction and self-awareness has various advantages In past professional development. It improves our lives and widens how we might interpret the world. By chasing after information and learning, we become all the more balanced people and are better prepared to deal with complex issues and pursue informed choices. Whether it is concentrating on craftsmanship, history, reasoning, or learning another dialect, training assists us with interfacing with various societies, social orders, and thoughts, giving us a more comprehensive perspective on the world.

Nonstop learning advances development and inventiveness. At the point when we open ourselves to new ideas, thoughts, and viewpoints, it invigorates our psyches and urges us to move toward issues and difficulties from elective points. By constantly learning, we foster a development outlook that permits us to consider new ideas, embrace change, and track down imaginative arrangements. In the present quickly developing world, imagination, and advancement are profoundly valued credits, and constant learning is an impetus for encouraging these characteristics.

In addition, putting resources into schooling and self-improvement emphatically influences our general prosperity. Learning new things and gaining new abilities has been displayed to work on psychological wellness and mental capability. It supports confidence, gives pride, and assists people with remaining mentally invigorated. Furthermore, constant learning energizes social communication and systems administration, as it frequently includes joining classes, going to courses, or partaking in studios. These social associations can play a critical part in our joy and generally life fulfillment.

Ceaseless learning and putting resources into training and self-awareness are crucial in the present high-speed and steadily impacting the world. It assists us with remaining significant in our vocations, adjusting to new difficulties, encouraging self-awareness, upgrading how we might interpret the world, advancing development, and working on by and large prosperity. By focusing on ceaseless learning, we put resources into ourselves and put ourselves in a good position in both our own and proficient lives. As the idiom goes, "The main thing that is consistent is change," and ceaseless learning furnishes us with the apparatuses to effectively explore this steady change.

12 Building strength and determination

Life is loaded with highs and lows. At times, we face difficulties that appear to be inconceivable and it tends to be not difficult to lose trust and feel crushed. Nonetheless, during these troublesome minutes building flexibility and diligence becomes urgent. Versatility is the capacity to recuperate rapidly from hardships and diligence is the faithfulness in accomplishing something regardless of deterrents or demoralization. These two characteristics remain closely connected and assume a critical part in assisting us not entirely set in stone during testing times. Building flexibility and diligence is certainly not an intrinsic quality; expertise can be created and refined after some time. Here are a few systems to assist you with developing these characteristics and remaining resolved while confronting difficulty:

1. **Acknowledgment and self-reflection:** The most vital move towards building versatility and constancy is acknowledging that demands and mishaps are a characteristic piece of life. Rather than harping on the negative viewpoints, consider what is happening dispassionately. Search for examples to gain and ponder how you can develop from the experience.

2. **Put forth sensible objectives:** During testing times, it tends to be overpowering to handle enormous undertakings or conquer significant snags at the same time. All things being equal, separate your objectives

into more modest, more sensible advances. This approach permits you to gain ground at a consistent speed and provides you with a feeling of achievement en route.

3. **Develop a positive mentality**: Your outlook assumes an urgent part in building versatility and constancy. Rather than zeroing in on the negative parts of a circumstance, attempt to track down the silver lining or search for the open doors for development. Practice appreciation and encircle yourself with positive impacts to keep your spirits high.

4. **Fabricate an emotionally supportive network**: Having areas of strength for a framework is indispensable while confronting testing times. Encircle yourself with individuals who inspire and rouse you. Look for direction from coaches or join support bunches where you can associate with other people who have confronted comparable difficulties. Sharing encounters and getting backing can furnish you with the solidarity to persist.

5. **Practice taking care of yourself**: Dealing with yourself truly, inwardly, and intellectually is fundamental for building flexibility and determination. Make a point to get sufficient rest, eat nutritious feasts, and participate in exercises that give you pleasure and unwinding. Take part in practices like contemplation, workouts, or journaling to assist with overseeing pressure and keeping on track.

6. **Embrace disappointment as a learning potential open door:** Disappointment is a fundamental piece of development and improvement. Instead of being deterred by mishaps, use them as a chance to learn, adjust, and get to the next level. Embrace disappointments as venturing stones to progress and allow them to fuel your assurance to continue to push forward.

7. **Keep a drawn-out point of view:** While confronting testing times, it is fundamental to recall that difficulties are impermanent. Keep a drawn-out point of view and help yourself to remember your definitive objectives and interests. Try not to neglect to focus on your fantasies and

goals, and use them as a wellspring of inspiration not entirely set in stone and persist.

8. **Practice versatility-building works out**: Very much like our actual muscles, flexibility, and steadiness can be reinforced through training. Take part in practices that challenge your strength, like defining little objectives and reliably pursuing them, or purposely presenting yourself to awkward circumstances. These activities assist with developing mental fortitude and increment your capacity to deal with affliction.

9. **Look for proficient assistance when vital**: At times, the difficulties we face might be overpowering, and we might need proficient support. There is no disgrace in looking for treatment or guidance to assist with exploring through troublesome times. Experts can give direction, backing, and apparatuses to foster strength and constancy.

PART 4: DEVELOPING AN OVERFLOW ATTITUDE

13 Appreciation as a flourishing magnet

In a world that frequently appears to be driven by the quest for progress, riches, and overflow, people are continually looking for ways of upgrading their lives. While there are numerous strategies and tactics, gratitude is a powerful yet frequently overlooked tool for attracting prosperity. The act of appreciation has been perceived for quite a long time as a groundbreaking power, for individual prosperity as well as a magnet for overflow. In this chapter, we dive into the significant association between appreciation and success, investigating how developing a mentality of gratefulness can prepare for a daily existence wealthy in overflow.

The Idea of Appreciation: A lasting feeling of appreciation is not enough to express gratitude; it is a mentality, a cognizant decision to recognize and value the positive parts of life. At its center, appreciation includes perceiving the decency that exists in one's life and paying little mind to outside conditions. This change in context can significantly affect generally speaking prosperity, making a gradually expanding influence that reaches out a long way past the quick second.

Connection Between Gratitude and Abundance: There is a connection between gratitude and abundance; Practicing gratitude has become increasingly prominent in scientific research. Various examinations have shown that people who consistently offer thanks experience lower levels of pressure, work on psychological wellness, and expand by and large life fulfillment. By fostering a sense of contentment and an openness to receiving more, this upbeat outlook attracts prosperity.

Celebrate triumphs of all shapes and sizes:

Along your excursion, make sure to commend your triumphs, regardless of how little they might appear. Perceive and recognize your advancement and accomplishments, as this will upgrade your inspiration and support your assurance during testing times. Creating strength and determination takes time and exertion. It requires a change in outlook and the eagerness to continue in any event, whenever troubles arise. By acknowledging demands, laying out practical objectives, and developing a positive mentality, you can fabricate strength not entirely set in stone during the most difficult times. Keep in mind, that versatility develops further through misfortune, and tirelessness is the fuel that keeps you pushing ahead.

Practical ways to cultivate gratitude include the following:

Journaling Your Gratitude: A simple but effective practice is keeping a gratitude journal. Every day, take a couple of seconds to ponder and record things you are grateful for. This interaction not only assists you with zeroing in on the positive parts of your life but also fills in as a strong sign of the overflow that as of now exists.

Expressing Appreciation: Expressing or composing articulations of appreciation to others can develop your feeling of appreciation. Not only does it make relationships stronger, but it also generates a positive energy that brings in more good things and abundance.

Positive Appreciation: Integrate care into your everyday daily schedule by being completely present at the time and valuing the little delights of life. This could incorporate enjoying some espresso, partaking in the dusk, or savoring a basic discussion.

Appreciation Reflection: Meditation on gratitude can help you develop a profound sense of appreciation. Allow feelings of gratitude to permeate your consciousness by focusing on the positive aspects of your life.

The Flourishing Magnet Impact: As people reliably practice appreciation, an unobtrusive yet strong shift happens in their impression of the world. The mentality of overflow replaces shortage, establishing a climate helpful for drawing in greater thriving.

Gratitude attracts prosperity in the following ways:

Attraction of Positive Energy: Positive energy is exuded from gratitude, bringing more opportunities and experiences into one's life. This vibrational shift adjusts people to the recurrence of overflow, making it more probable for them to draw in flourishing.

Being open to receiving: Appreciation develops a receptiveness to getting and recognizing the overflow that encompasses us. As people become more sensitive to the positive parts of their lives, they become more responsive to valuable open doors for development and achievement.

General rule that good energy attracts good: The pattern of good following good sets that like draws in like. Appreciation, as a positive and thankful power, adjusts people to the energy of overflow, making it more likely that they will draw in comparative positive encounters.

Upgraded Navigation: A thankful mentality improves mental capabilities, prompting better independent direction. Clear and positive decisions add to the general direction of one's life, directing people towards open doors that advance thriving.

Recognizing gratitude's power as a powerful attractor of abundance is essential in the pursuit of prosperity. Our perception of the world and the very fabric of our experiences are both altered when we intentionally practice gratitude. People cultivate the conditions necessary for prosperity to take root and flourish by modeling appreciation. We can unlock the door to a life that is enriched by abundance in all of its forms if we embrace gratitude as a prosperity magnet.

14 The pattern of good following good

Understanding and applying its principles for financial success The Law of Attraction states that like attracts like and that our thoughts can shape our reality. This is a principle that has received a lot of attention in recent years. The Law of Attraction is a potent force that extends its influence to the realm of financial success, even though it is frequently associated with personal development and well-being. This chapter delves into the fundamental tenets of the Law of Attraction and demonstrates how comprehending and applying these tenets can open the door to financial prosperity.

The Importance of Pattern of Energy Attracting Similar Energy

The basic idea behind the Law of Attraction is that the energy we put out, whether we are aware of it or not, attracts similar energy into our lives. This all inclusive rule works on the conviction that considerations are strong magnets, drawing in conditions, individuals, and encounters that reverberate with the vibrational recurrence of those contemplations.

Consistent focus: The most important phase in tackling the Pattern of good following good for monetary achievement is acquiring clearness about your monetary objectives. Characterize what you need to accomplish, whether it's a particular pay level, monetary freedom, or the acknowledgment of a specific monetary desire. The more exact and distinctive your considerations, the more engaged the energy you discharge.

Positive Perception: The Law of Attraction relies heavily on visualization.

37

Think in detail about your financial success and the feelings, experiences, and outcomes that come with achieving your goals. Perception builds up your positive contemplations as well as adjusts your psyche brain to your cognizant longings.

Insistences and Positive Language: Create positive attestations that certify your monetary achievement. Use language that bolsters your belief in prosperity and abundance. Rehash these attestations consistently, permitting them to become imbued in your psyche and mind and affecting your general outlook toward monetary achievement.

Appreciation as an Impetus: The Law of Attraction gains more traction when people are grateful. No matter how modest your current financial situation is, acknowledge it and express gratitude. Appreciation fills in as a magnet for additional positive encounters, making the way for expanded overflow.

Financial Success Using the Law of Attraction: The first step is to comprehend the Law of Attraction's fundamentals; executing these standards into your day-to-day routine is where groundbreaking wizardry occurs.

Positive Monetary Outlook: Develop a positive outlook about cash. Think about abundance and prosperity rather than scarcity and lack. By intentionally picking positive considerations about your monetary circumstance, you adjust your energy to the overflow you look for.

Adjusting Activities to Goals: The Law of Attraction encompasses more than just thoughts; It all comes down to matching your actions with your goals. Make a roused move toward your monetary objectives. This could mean looking for new opportunities, making smart investments, or learning new skills that help you make more money.

Encircling Yourself with Inspiration: Your energy is greatly influenced by your surroundings. Encircle yourself with positive impacts, whether it's steady people, inspirational substance, or an elevating actual space. The energy of abundance is bolstered and amplified by positive surroundings.

Discharge Restricting Convictions: Distinguish and deliver any restricting convictions about cash and achievement. These convictions frequently go about as obstructions to the progression of overflow. Replace limiting beliefs with ones that are empowering and in line with your financial objectives by becoming aware of yourself and making an effort to do so.

Keeping Your Patience and Perseverance: The Pattern of energy attracting similar energy works time permitting outline. Both patience and persistent effort toward your financial goals are essential. Trust the cycle, keep fixed on your objectives, and stay open to surprising open doors that might line up with your desires.

Success Stories and Case Studies: The transformative power of the Law of Attraction in the realm of financial success is demonstrated by numerous success stories. People who have embraced the standards of positive reasoning, perception, and appreciation frequently report critical upgrades in their monetary circumstances.

Affirmations for a Successful Business: Business professionals and entrepreneurs frequently attribute their success to the power of affirmations. They have developed a mindset that motivates them to take the necessary actions to achieve their goals by consistently affirming their belief in financial abundance and business success.

Gratitude and the Attraction of Wealth: Rehearsing appreciation has been a consistent theme among the individuals who have encountered huge monetary achievement. People have reported a noticeable increase in abundance and prosperity by expressing gratitude for their current financial situation and opportunities. In the excursion toward monetary achievement, understanding and utilizing the standards of the Pattern of good following good can be a distinct advantage. By adjusting your contemplations, feelings, and activities with the energy of overflow, you make a strong magnet that brings monetary thriving into your life. The Pattern of good following good fills in as a core value, advising us that our mentality and convictions assume a vital part in molding our monetary reality. As you leave on the way to monetary achievement, recall that the energy you emanate into the universe can possibly shape your monetary predetermination, making the Pattern of good following good a strong power chasing flourishing.

15 Relinquishing shortage attitude

In a world frequently portrayed by contest, correlation, and the feeling of dread toward need, numerous people wind up caught in a shortage mindset — a mentality that trusts assets, potential open doors, and achievement are restricted. Nonetheless, the way to genuine thriving starts with a crucial change in context. This change includes relinquishing the viewpoint that everything is limited and embracing overflow and abundance awareness. In this chapter, we dive into the underlying foundations of shortage mindset, its effect on our lives, and the enabling excursion toward developing an outlook that draws in overflow and riches.

Figuring out Shortage Mindset: Shortage mindset, established in the anxiety toward deficiency, appears as a conviction that there isn't sufficient to go around. This outlook is portrayed by sensations of need, rivalry, and a consistent correlation with others. People grasped by shortage mindset frequently approach existence with a feeling of dread, uneasiness, and a fundamental conviction that valuable open doors are restricted, making achievement slippery.

Starting points of Shortage Mindset: Shortage attitude can follow its underlying foundations to different sources, including youth encounters, cultural molding, and social impacts. Messages of shortage might have been imbued through childhood, monetary difficulties, or openness to a culture that stresses contest over coordinated effort.

The Effect on Prosperity: Living with a world view limited by fear can significantly affect one's general prosperity. It makes pressure, uneasiness, and a steady insecurity. This outlook might prompt behaving

41

destructively ways of behaving, botched open doors, and stressed connections as people work from a position of dread instead of overflow.

Unavoidable outcome: The tricky idea of shortage mindset lies in its capacity to turn into an inevitable outcome. Having faith in shortage frequently restricts one's capacity to perceive and jump all over chances, building up the very conditions that are dreaded. Breaking liberated from this cycle requires a cognizant work to move one's viewpoint.

Embracing Overflow and Abundance Cognizance: The excursion toward embracing overflow and abundance awareness includes overhauling firmly established convictions and cultivating a mentality that sees prospects, celebrates achievement, and has confidence in the innate wealth of life.

Mindfulness and Awareness: The initial move toward change is mindfulness. Perceive when shortage considerations emerge, and carefully notice the thought processes that add to the mentality of need. Mindfulness makes the space for change by permitting people to deliberately pick contemplations that line up with overflow.

Appreciation as an Impetus: Appreciation fills in as a strong counteractant to shortage mindset. By moving the concentration based on the thing is missing to what is available, people open themselves to the overflow that as of now exists in their lives. Standard appreciation practice develops a positive outlook and draws in additional purposes behind appreciation..

Flood Viewpoint Affirmations: Positive confirmations are expected to a basic part in reshaping conviction structures. Make affirmations that reflect an overflow perspective, such as "I genuinely deserve success," "Open doors flow to me easily," or "I'm surrounded by overflow in all parts of my life." Consistently recite these certifications to back up your positive convictions.

Overflow Guides and Good examples: Encircle yourself with people who epitomize an overflow outlook. Gain from guides and good examples who have effectively risen above shortage thinking and accomplished monetary overflow. Their accounts and viewpoints can rouse and direct you on your own excursion.

Beating Shortage Blocks: Relinquishing shortage mindset requires a guarantee to self-improvement and an eagerness to challenge profoundly imbued convictions. Here are systems to beat shortage blocks and make ready for overflow:

Re-evaluate Difficulties as Any open doors: Rather than considering difficulties to be road obstructions, view them as any open doors for development and learning. A change in context changes snags into venturing stones toward progress.

Observe Others Prosperity: Instead of surrendering to envy or rivalry, praise the progress of others. Perceive that their accomplishments don't lessen your own true capacity for progress. Embracing an outlook of cooperation cultivates a feeling of solidarity and shared overflow.

Put resources into Self-improvement: Focus on persistent self-awareness. Put time and assets in obtaining new abilities, extending your insight, and improving your capacities. A mentality zeroed in on development and learning is intrinsically lined up with overflow.

Discharge the Feeling of dread toward Disappointment: Anxiety toward disappointment is a typical part of shortage thinking. Embrace disappointment as a characteristic piece of the growing experience and a chance for course remedy. Every misfortune brings important examples and draws you nearer to progress.

Practice Liberality: Effectively take part in demonstrations of liberality and graciousness. The demonstration of giving, whether through time, assets, or backing, encourages a feeling of overflow and supports the conviction that there is all that could possibly be needed to share.

From Monetary Battle to Overflow: Stories flourish of people who, regardless of confronting monetary difficulties, changed their attitude and pulled in overflow. By embracing an overflow outlook, developing appreciation, and making roused moves, they turned their monetary circumstances around and made uncommon progress.

Business people Embracing Overflow: Business people frequently share accounts of changing from a viewpoint that everything is limited to one of overflow. By zeroing in on development, coordinated effort, and a confidence in limitless potential outcomes, they have fabricated fruitful organizations that flourish in an outlook of overflow.

The excursion from shortage mindset to overflow and abundance cognizance is a significant and groundbreaking interaction. It includes a purposeful change in mentality, overhauling firmly established convictions, and embracing the innate wealth of life. As people let go of the anxiety toward need, they open themselves to a universe of conceivable outcomes, draw in potential open doors, and manifest monetary achievement. The way to overflow isn't simply a change in conditions however a significant inward change that emanates into each part of life. By deciding to embrace overflow and abundance cognizance, people prepare for a future set apart by thriving, satisfaction, and a profound appreciation for the lavishness of life's contributions

16 Encircling yourself with similar people and coaches

Encircling oneself with similar people and coaches isn't just a social decision; an essential choice can fundamentally influence one's way of living. In this investigation, we dig into the significant force of lining up with similar companions and looking for direction from guides, analyzing how these associations add to self-improvement, objective accomplishment, and by and large satisfaction.

The Impact of Similar People

Shared Values and Objectives: Similar people share normal qualities, desires, and objectives. By encircling yourself with individuals who reverberate with your convictions and targets, you establish a strong climate where everybody is making progress toward a common vision. This common feeling of direction cultivates cooperation, motivation, and an aggregate drive for progress.

Positive Energy and Inspiration: Similar people emanate positive energy and inspiration. Their energy and excitement become infectious, rousing every individual from the gathering to take a stab at greatness. The aggregate force made by such a positive air can drive everybody towards more significant levels of accomplishment.

Shared Help and Responsibility: Building associations with similar companions makes an organization of common help and responsibility. Whether chasing after private objectives, proficient undertakings, or a mix of both, having a local area that empowers and considers each other responsible improves the probability of progress.

Variety of Points of view: While similar people share shared objectives, they might offer different viewpoints and encounters that would be useful. This variety improves the aggregate figuring out, empowering innovativeness and advancement. The trading of thoughts inside such a gathering can prompt balanced independent direction and critical thinking.

Flexibility Despite Difficulties: Similar people offer areas of strength for a framework during testing times. While confronting deterrents or misfortunes, the aggregate assurance and consolation of the gathering can support individual versatility. This common strength assists everybody with exploring difficulties with a positive and arrangement situated outlook.

The Job of Coaches in Private and Expert Turn of Events

Direction from Experienced People: Coaches, by definition, are people with additional experience and skill in a specific field. Conforming to a tutor gives admittance to important directions and experiences that can speed up your expectation to learn and adapt. Their insight and firsthand experience offer a guide for exploring difficulties and jumping all over chances.

Sped-up Mastering and Expertise Improvement: Tutors assume a vital part in speeding up mastering and ability improvement. Through direct collaboration, mentorship gives customized direction, useful criticism, and reasonable exhortation. This designated help can essentially upgrade your capacities and abilities.

Extended Organization and Open Doors: Guides frequently have broad organizations in their particular enterprises. By being tutored, you get sufficiently close to this organization, opening ways to important associations and valuable open doors. The coach-mentee relationship can act as an extension to new organizations, joint efforts, and expert connections.

Certainty Building: Having a coach who trusts in your true capacity can help your certainty. Their consolation and certification add to a positive mental self-portrait, engaging you to take on difficulties and seek after aggressive objectives. The guide's faith in your capacities can be a main thrust for conquering self-question.

Long haul Point of view and Key Preparation: Guides give a drawn out viewpoint that stretches out past quick difficulties. Their experience permits them to anticipate likely entanglements and guide you in essential preparation. This forward-looking methodology guarantees that your endeavors line up with more extensive objectives and add to supported achievement.

Procedures for Developing Significant Associations:

Recognize Shared Interests and Values: Effectively search out people who share your inclinations and values. Go to systems administration occasions, join clubs or associations, and partake in networks where you are probably going to experience similar companions. A shared view gives a strong groundwork for building significant associations.

Be Available to Assorted Viewpoints: While looking for similar people, stay open to different points of view. Contrasts in foundation, encounters, and sentiments can improve your comprehension and add to a more unique and imaginative climate.

Use Online Stages: Influence online stages and networks to associate with similar people. Online entertainment, discussions, and expert systems administration locales offer chances to draw in individuals who share your interests and objectives, paying little heed to geological limits.

Look for Tutors Proactively: Effectively search out guides who have made progress in regions you seek to investigate. Go to industry occasions, connect through proficient organizations, and express certifiable interest in gaining from their encounters. Proactivity in looking for mentorship exhibits your development obligation.

Take part in Brains Gatherings: Genius gatherings, where people with different abilities and foundations meet up to help one another, can be a strong discussion for joint effort. These gatherings encourage aggregate critical thinking, responsibility, and shared achievement.

Innovative Accomplishment through Mentorship: Numerous effective business people characteristic a critical piece of their prosperity to mentorship. By lining up with experienced coaches who gave direction on business systems, organizing, and conquering difficulties, these business visionaries had the option to explore the intricacies of the business world more.

Imaginative Joint Effort in Human Expression: In innovative businesses, specialists, essayists, and artists frequently structure cooperative organizations of similar people. By cooperating, sharing thoughts, and offering valuable input, they establish a climate that sustains imagination and speeds up creative turn of events.

The force of encircling yourself with similar people and looking for direction from tutors couldn't possibly be more significant. These purposeful associations shape your current conditions as well as the direction of your future. Similar friends give a strong local area, encouraging cooperation, inspiration, and shared achievement. Coaches, with their abundance of involvement, offer important direction, speed up learning, and give a guide to accomplishing your objectives. As you set out on your excursion of individual and expert development, think about the impact of people around you. Develop associations with people who share your qualities and objectives, and effectively search out guides who can give bits of knowledge and backing. In the embroidery of your life, these associations weave strings of motivation, versatility, and accomplishment, making a material on which your goals can unfurl and thrive.

PART 5: PROCEEDING WITH POTENTIALLY DANGEROUS COURSES OF ACTION AND EMBRACING DISAPPOINTMENT

17 Understanding Gamble versus Prize in Abundance Creation

In the realm of money and effective financial planning, the idea of hazard is an urgent component that each financial backer requires to comprehend. The capacity to ascertain and oversee risk is fundamental in abundance creation. Understanding the connection between hazard and prize can assist people with settling on informed venture choices and working on their possibilities to make monetary progress.

Before digging into the complexities of ascertaining risk, appreciating the basics of chance and reward is fundamental. In basic terms, risk alludes to the likelihood or probability of speculation or adventure not proceeding true to form. Then again, reward means the possible return or gain that an individual could accomplish from a specific venture. These two ideas are inherently connected and structure the premise of abundance creation.

Concerning evaluating risk, a few variables become an integral factor. One of the essential components is grasping the actual venture. This implies directing exhaustive examination and investigation to acquire bits of knowledge into the speculation's hidden essentials, financials, and economic situations. A very educated financial backer has a higher opportunity to precisely evaluate the gamble related to a specific speculation or adventure.

One more basic part of working out risk is assessing the authentic exhibition of comparative speculations or adventures. This examination gives a benchmark against which the ongoing venture can measure up. It empowers financial backers to measure the potential dangers in light of authentic patterns and examples, assisting them with pursuing more educated choices.

Moreover, evaluating risk likewise implies thinking about outer factors like financial circumstances, administrative changes, and international occasions that might influence speculation. These outer impacts can essentially influence the presentation and strength of ventures, making extra dangers that should be figured into the gamble estimation process. When the gamble related to a venture has been recognized, the following stage is to decide the possible prize. This includes working out the normal profit from the venture (return for money invested) and gauging it against the dangers recognized before. Higher potential rewards frequently accompany higher dangers, while lower-risk ventures commonly yield lower returns. This harmony among chance and award is where the idea of hazard versus compensation in abundance creation becomes possibly the most important factor.

One generally involved technique for ascertaining hazard and prize is the Sharpe Proportion. This proportion assists financial backers with evaluating the return accomplished for how much gamble is taken. By breaking down a portfolio's or alternately speculation's verifiable execution, the Sharpe Proportion features whether the profits produced are similar to the degree of chance taken. This proportion permits financial backers to analyze various ventures and figure out which one gives the most alluring gamble to remunerate compromise.

The idea of hazard versus reward isn't simply restricted to individual speculations yet in addition applies to enhancement. Differentiating one's speculation portfolio across different resource classes and areas helps spread the gamble. By putting resources into various regions, people can diminish the effect of solitary speculation performing inadequately. The objective is to track down the right harmony between high-risk, high-reward ventures, and lower-risk, lower-reward resources for upgrade abundance creation.

Nonetheless, it is vital to note that hazard is an inborn piece of abundance creation. Without taking in some way or another of hazard, it becomes testing to accomplish huge monetary prizes. Computing risk, in this manner, includes finding some kind of harmony between alleviating exorbitant dangers while as yet chasing after possibly worthwhile open doors.

Understanding gamble versus reward is pivotal in abundance creation and speculation navigation. Working out risk implies assessing different elements, like the actual venture, verifiable execution, outer impacts, and expected rewards. The utilization of devices like the Sharpe Proportion can help with deciding the gamble to remunerate compromise and contrasting different venture choices. While risk is a fundamental thought, it is through well balanced plan of action that people can build their possibilities making monetary progress in the long haul.

18 Overcoming Dreads

Dread is a characteristic human feeling that can some of the time frustrate us from accomplishing our actual potential. With regards to funds, dread frequently shows itself in our hesitance to face challenges or take striking actions that could prompt monetary forward leaps. Notwithstanding, if we need to make progress and independence from the rat race, it is fundamental to defeat our apprehensions and make important strides toward accomplishing our objectives.

The most important phase in conquering dread is to perceive and recognize its presence. Dread can mask itself in different structures - apprehension about disappointment, anxiety toward progress, apprehension about vulnerability, and even a feeling of dread toward change. By recognizing our particular feelings of trepidation, we can go up against and address them head-on, rather than permitting them to control our activities.

Whenever we have distinguished our apprehensions, we can begin dealing with altering our outlook. Dread frequently comes according to a negative viewpoint and a conviction that we are not equipped to accomplish our monetary objectives. To beat this, we want to rethink our contemplations and spotlight certain attestations. By letting ourselves know that we are fit and meriting monetary achievement, we can gradually really impact our outlook and foster a more certain and brave demeanor.

Making striking strides toward a monetary leap forward requires getting out of our usual ranges of familiarity. We frequently become alright with our ongoing monetary circumstance, regardless of whether it isn't great.

This solace can hold us back from wandering into new open doors or proceeding with carefully weighed-out courses of action that might prompt a leap forward. Breaking liberated from the chains of solace requires a cognizant choice to propel ourselves past our cutoff points and investigate additional opportunities.

One powerful method for defeating our apprehensions and making striking strides towards monetary forward leaps is by laying out clear and reasonable objectives. Objectives furnish us with an internal compass and reason, and they can act as an inspiration for us to defeat our feelings of trepidation. By putting forth unmistakable and quantifiable objectives, we can isolate our excursion toward monetary accomplishment into more modest, achievable advances. This approach permits us to zero in on gaining consistent headway without becoming overpowered by the 10,000-foot view.

One more significant part of conquering dread is to fabricate a steady organization of similar people. Encircling ourselves with individuals who share comparable objectives and goals can give us the support and inspiration expected to make strong strides toward a monetary leap forward. This organization can offer counsel, direction, and moral help, particularly during times when trepidation could attempt to pull us back.

Moreover, looking for information and training can likewise assist us with conquering our apprehensions. Frequently, dread stems from an absence of understanding or information in a specific region, like ventures or business. By focusing on learning and acquiring ability, we can help our certainty and feel more equipped to pursue informed choices. Schooling can come in different structures, whether it is reading books, going to classes, or in any event, getting proficient affirmations.

Making striking strides towards monetary forward leaps additionally requires tolerance and diligence. Dread can make us become fretful, anticipating moment results. In any case, it is crucial to comprehend that monetary achievement requires some investment and exertion. By staying relentless and focused on our objectives, even notwithstanding deterrents or mishaps, we can ultimately get through our feelings of trepidation and accomplish the forward leaps we want.

Rehearsing appreciation and being thankful for what we now have can assist us with beating our feelings of trepidation. Dread frequently emerges from a viewpoint that everything is limited, where we center around what we need or dread losing. By moving our concentration towards appreciation and recognizing the overflow in our lives, we can develop a more sure and bold outlook. Appreciation permits us to see the value in the headway we have created and the open doors that lie ahead, advising us that making strong strides towards monetary leap forwards merits the gamble.

Defeating dread is a fundamental stage toward accomplishing a monetary leap forward. By perceiving our feelings of trepidation, rethinking our mentality, getting out of our usual ranges of familiarity, putting forth clear objectives, fabricating a strong organization, looking for information and training, rehearsing tolerance and ingenuity, and developing appreciation, we can overcome our feelings of dread and leave on an excursion towards monetary achievement. Keep in mind, making striking strides isn't tied in with wiping out dread altogether, but about recognizing it and deciding to push ahead notwithstanding it.

19 Gaining from Disappointment and Transforming Difficulties into Venturing Stones

Disappointment is an inescapable piece of life. It can be crippling, upsetting, and demotivating. However, the ability to learn from failure and use setbacks as stepping stones to success sets successful people apart from others. History is weighed down with accounts of incredible characters who experienced various disappointments before accomplishing their objectives. A powerful mindset that can lead to personal and professional success embraces failure as a learning opportunity and sees it as an opportunity to improve and evolve.

One of the vital parts of gaining from disappointment is embracing a development mentality. Instead of overview frustration as a keep going choice on one's abilities or worth, seeing it as an opportunity for improvement and improvement is huge. "Disappointment is an outcome in the works," was stated by Albert Einstein. Stating from the point of view, each disappointment fills in as a venturing stone toward progress since it shows important illustrations and gives criticism that can assist with driving ensuing undertakings. Furthermore, failure frequently provides insights that success cannot. It forces individuals to examine their actions, strategies, and improvement opportunities. People are better able to comprehend what went wrong and how they can avoid similar obstacles in the future by analyzing the mistakes they made. Because they improve one's capacity for resilience, adaptability, and problem-solving skills, these insights become invaluable resources for both personal and professional growth.

In addition, failing teaches valuable life lessons like humility, perseverance, and the capacity to triumph over difficulties. It forces people to face their limitations, acknowledge their weaknesses, and acknowledge areas in which they can improve. Through this contemplation, people foster a superior comprehension of themselves, expanding mindfulness and personal development. In addition, failure fosters resilience because it forces people to face difficulties and obstacles that require them to recover and keep moving forward.

Transforming misfortunes into venturing stones additionally includes reexamining the story around disappointment. Rather than seeing disappointment as an individual blemish or an impasse, it ought to be viewed as a venturing stone towards progress. "Think like a queen," Oprah Winfrey, a well-known media mogul, once advised. A sovereign won't hesitate to fizzle. Another step toward greatness is failure. People can turn setbacks into opportunities for growth and self-improvement by changing how they see failure.

Additionally, experiencing setbacks and failure can cultivate an entrepreneurial spirit. Before experiencing breakthrough success, many successful entrepreneurs have experienced multiple failures. They comprehend that disappointment is an inborn piece of the innovative excursion, and the people who embrace it are bound to succeed. These misfortunes become illustrations that shape their pioneering outlook, showing them how to construct strength, turn techniques, and continue despite impediments.

Gaining from disappointment likewise requires a change in context towards botches. Mistakes shouldn't be viewed as something to be ashamed of; rather, they should be viewed as opportunities for learning. One of history's greatest inventors, Thomas Edison, once said, "I have not failed." I've just discovered 10,000 ineffective methods." The significance of using mistakes as stepping stones to success is demonstrated by Edison's unwavering pursuit of success through trial and error.

In addition, being willing to persevere is necessary for learning from mistakes and turning setbacks into opportunities. It is vital to push through disillusionment, misfortunes, and even criticism to continue to push ahead. The way to progress is seldom straight; it is loaded up with diversions, impediments, and disappointments. The people who endure despite affliction are bound to accomplish their objectives over the long haul.

Finally, looking for help and direction is essential while gaining from disappointment. Encircling oneself with an organization of coaches, companions, and partners who can give direction, offer counsel, and their encounters can speed up the expectation to learn and adapt. These people can give important experiences, points of view, and consolation while confronting difficulties, assisting with changing disappointments into venturing stones towards progress.

Gaining from disappointment and transforming misfortunes into venturing stones is a strong mentality that can possibly lead people to individual and expert achievement. When faced with failure, key traits to cultivate include adopting a growth mindset, analyzing failures for lessons learned, reframing the narrative, accepting mistakes, persevering, and seeking support. Individuals can transform setbacks into opportunities for growth, learning, and ultimately success by approaching failure with resilience, persistence, and a thirst for knowledge.

20 The significance of diligence and flexibility

Life is a progression of highs and lows, and it is at times of misfortune that the ideals of diligence and flexibility sparkle. Envision yourself strolling on a way, loaded up with deterrents and difficulties. You stumble and fall on the way. What you do next becomes crucial at that point. Will you capitulate to misery and surrender, or will you embrace the force of determination and flexibility and rise once more? In this section, we dig into the meaning of getting oneself after a fall and investigate how these excellencies add to self-improvement, accomplishment, and at last, achievement.

1. **Beating misfortunes:** Difficulties are an inescapable piece of life. They can come in different structures like disappointments, dismissals, or dissatisfactions. Nonetheless, it isn't the actual misfortunes but our reaction to them that decides our future achievement. Steadiness and strength go about as the light power that keeps us above water in violent times. By embracing these ethics, we figure out how to see difficulties as any open doors for development and improvement instead of as inconceivable hindrances.

2. **Fostering a development mentality:** We can develop a growth mindset thanks to our resilience and perseverance. When confronted with disappointment, people with a development mentality comprehend that their capacities can be created through commitment and difficult work. They view moves as open doors to grow their abilities and information, as opposed to being hindered by transitory misfortunes. We foster a sense of continuous self-development by picking ourselves up after a fall, which bolsters our motivation to learn and grow.

3. **Developing inward fortitude**: Getting ourselves after a fall requires inward strength and conviction. It helps us to depend on our versatility as opposed to tracking down outer wellsprings of help. Through the course of self-reflection and confidence, we foster an unflinching faith in our capacities to handle any difficulties that come our direction. In addition, this inner strength becomes a valuable asset that enables us to overcome challenges in the future with self-assurance and determination.

4. **Divulging stowed away potential:** Frequently, after a fall, we find stowed away qualities and gifts inside ourselves that might have in any case stayed torpid. Tirelessness and flexibility push us to take advantage of our maximum capacity, as we figure out how to push past our usual ranges of familiarity and embrace distress. We discover our hidden abilities, creativity, and resilience during these trying times, resulting in personal development and transformation.

5. **Motivating others:** Our capacity to get ourselves after a fall can be a strong wellspring of motivation for everyone around us. We demonstrate the significance of resilience as a crucial component of success through our actions. We encourage others to overcome obstacles and demonstrate perseverance. Our resilience has the potential to spread, creating a community that is resolute and motivated to achieve greatness like a wave.

6. **Making long-haul progress:** Achievement isn't effortlessly accomplished; it requires consistent exertion and the capacity to persevere through difficulties. It is more likely that people will achieve their long-term objectives if they have resilience and perseverance. By declining to surrender, they continue even with difficulty and show the perseverance important to conquer impediments. They are willing to put in the necessary time and effort to achieve their goals because they know that success is a marathon, not a sprint.

In this present reality where moment satisfaction is often looked for, the ideals of steadiness and strength are turning out to be progressively significant. When we pick ourselves up from a fall, we realize that we can overcome obstacles, cultivate a growth mindset, cultivate inner strength, reveal hidden potential, motivate others, and, in the end, achieve long-term success. Therefore, the next time you stumble and fall, keep in mind the significance of perseverance and resilience—these are the forces that will assist you in rising to the occasion and conquering the obstacles that lie ahead of you.

PART 6: LEAVING AN ENDURING LEGACY

21 Leaving a positive effect on the world

In a world loaded with difficulties, utilizing privately invested money to make a positive effect has turned into a strong and groundbreaking methodology. The idea of magnanimity has developed past conventional foundation, with people presently trying to add to tackling worldwide issues effectively. This section investigates the different manners by which abundance can be utilized to have a significant and enduring effect on the planet.

Figuring out the Influence of Riches: Riches, when employed capably, can be a power for huge great. Past private solace and extravagance, furnishes people with the chance to impact positive change for a bigger scope. The acknowledgment that abundance accompanies an obligation to society has driven numerous effective people to take on an outlook of generosity.

Vital Generosity: Charity includes an insightful and intentional way to deal with giving, zeroing in on making reasonable answers for cultural issues. As opposed to just making one-time gifts, people are progressively effective money management time and assets to comprehend the underlying drivers of issues, empowering them to make educated and significant commitments.

Areas of Effect:

1. **Schooling:** Putting resources into instruction is broadly perceived as one of the best ways of achieving positive change. By supporting

instructive drives, people can engage people in the future with the information and abilities important to handle worldwide difficulties.

2. **Medical care:** Dispensing assets to medical services further develops admittance to clinical consideration, exploration, and sickness anticipation. This substantially affects networks, upgrading generally speaking prosperity and life span.

3. **Natural Preservation:** Resolving ecological issues is essential for the prosperity of our planet. Abundance can be coordinated towards projects zeroed in on supportability, environmentally friendly power, and protection endeavors, adding to a better and more maintainable future.

4. **Destitution Mitigation:** Abundance can be a useful asset in the battle against neediness. By supporting drives that give financial open doors, admittance to assets, and the ability to prepare, people can assist with breaking the pattern of neediness in networks all over the planet.

5. **Civil rights:** Pushing for civil rights and fairness is another region where abundance can have a huge effect. Supporting associations that work towards killing segregation, advancing common freedoms, and addressing foundational treacheries can add to a fair and evenhanded society.

Cooperative Methodologies: Numerous givers are perceiving the significance of joint effort in amplifying their effect. By cooperating with similar people, associations, and legislatures, they can pool assets, share information, and make collaborations that lead to additional compelling and supportable arrangements.

The Job of Innovation: In the computerized age, innovation assumes an urgent part in enhancing the effect of magnanimity. Stages for crowdfunding, online entertainment mindfulness crusades, and advanced developments have made it simpler for people to interface with and support causes that impact them.

The Significance of Effect Estimation: To guarantee that abundance is utilized actually, estimating the effect of altruistic efforts is critical. Taking on measurements and assessment processes assists givers with grasping the results of their speculations, considering consistent improvement and refinement of procedures.

In a world confronting complex difficulties, the positive effect of utilizing abundance to have an effect couldn't possibly be more significant. Whether through essential generosity, cooperative endeavors, or utilizing innovation, people can add to enduring change. By coordinating assets towards training, medical services, ecological preservation, destitution lightening, and civil rights, abundance turns into an impetus for progress, cultivating a more splendid and more fair future for all.

22 Charity and the significance of social obligation

In a world set apart by different difficulties and differences, the idea of offering back has arisen as a strong power for positive change. Magnanimity, characterized as the affection for mankind, and social obligation, the affirmation of an individual or association's obligation to add to the prosperity of society, assume fundamental parts in molding an additional fair and caring world. This part dives into the meaning of generosity and the significance of social obligation in cultivating economic and positive effects on networks.

The Importance of Generosity:

Magnanimity goes past simple monetary gifts; it includes a comprehensive obligation to work on the human condition. It includes the deliberate arrangement of assets — be now is the right time, mastery, or monetary capital — toward makes that look for address cultural issues and inspire networks. Givers, driven by a feeling of sympathy and obligation, effectively participate in drives that make enduring and significant changes.

The Development of Social Obligation: Social obligation, in both individual and corporate settings, has developed as an ethical objective. In past benefit-making, organizations and people perceived their jobs as partners in the more extensive social texture. This development originates from a comprehension that a flourishing society is complicatedly connected to the prosperity of its singular individuals, and hence, adding to the benefit of everyone is a common obligation.

Key Parts of Social Obligation:

1. **Moral Strategic approaches:** For partnerships, social obligation starts with moral strategic policies. This incorporates fair work rehearses, natural manageability, and straightforward dealings. Organizations that focus on moral lead add to the formation of a business climate that values respectability and responsibility.

2. **Local area Commitment:** People and associations are progressively understanding the significance of effectively captivating the networks where they work. This includes putting resources into nearby drives, supporting local area improvement tasks, and encouraging associations with grassroots associations to address explicit necessities.

3. **Natural Stewardship:** Perceiving the effect of human exercises on the climate, social obligation reaches out to ecological stewardship. Organizations and people the same are taking on reasonable work on, diminishing their carbon impression, and supporting drives that advance natural protection.

4. **Variety and Consideration:** Social obligation incorporates a guarantee of variety and consideration. Organizations that worth and advance variety make comprehensive working environments, cultivate development, and add to a general public that celebrates contrasts as opposed to propagates imbalance.

The Job of Charity in Friendly Obligation: Magnanimity fills in as an unmistakable articulation of social obligation. Whether through individual thoughtful gestures or enormous-scope institutional giving, altruism gives the resources to resolve squeezing social issues. By supporting causes connected with training, medical care, and destitution easing, and that's only the tip of the iceberg, givers add to the formation of an additional equitable and sympathetic world.

The Significance of Cooperation: The main effect frequently emerges from cooperative endeavors. Social obligation is amplified when people, organizations, and states meet up to address foundational challenges.

Cooperative drives can use assorted viewpoints, assets, and ability to foster far-reaching and economical arrangements.

Estimating Effect and Responsibility: To guarantee the adequacy of charity and social obligation drives, laying out measurements for influence measurement is vital. Humanitarians and socially dependable elements are progressively centered around defining clear objectives, following results, and staying responsible for the networks they mean to serve.

In a worldwide scene set apart by interconnected difficulties, the standards of generosity and social obligation stand as encouraging signs. By rewarding society, whether through monetary commitments, local area commitment, or moral strategic policies, people and associations add to the production of a more caring, evenhanded, and feasible world. Perceiving the intrinsic interconnectedness of mankind, embracing charity, and recognizing the significance of social obligation prepare for a more brilliant and more comprehensive future for all.

23 Leaving a legacy for future generations

A common objective of many individuals and families is to ensure generational wealth transfer and leave a lasting legacy for future generations. It includes insightful preparation, successful methodologies, and a solid obligation to saving riches and giving it to people in the future. We will examine the meaning of generational abundance move, the troubles it presents, and a few reasonable advances that can be taken to ensure the exchange of riches and the making of an enduring heritage in this chapter.

Generational abundance move alludes to the most common way of passing down aggregated abundance starting with one age then onto the next. It includes something beyond passing on monetary resources; it envelops passing on family values, customs, information, and open doors for people in the future to flourish. Beyond tangible assets, intangible assets like family history, education, and social responsibility are all part of the process of leaving a lasting legacy. Financial stability, opportunity, and security can all be improved by ensuring this transfer.

Notwithstanding, achieving generational abundance move can challenge. Studies and measurements have shown that a huge level of acquired abundance is much of the time wasted or lost inside a couple of ages. Deficient preparation, absence of monetary instruction, unfortunate correspondence, and unexpected conditions can all add to the disintegration of generational riches. Hence, it is essential to foster an extensive system to forestall this destiny and lay out an enduring inheritance for future relatives.

1. **Begin Early**: Planning in advance is one of the most crucial steps in ensuring the transfer of wealth is successful. Start by making a comprehensive estate plan that includes powers of attorney, trusts, and a will. This plan will direct the way that resources are conveyed and overseen in case of death or insufficiency. By beginning early, you have additional opportunity to refine your arrangement, address any expected issues, and make essential changes en route.

2. **Encourage Monetary Instruction:** Teaching people in the future about monetary issues is vital to effective abundance move. Show your kids and grandkids about the worth of cash, planning, money management, and domain arranging. Give open doors to them to learn and acquire active involvement with overseeing funds. It is fundamental to furnish them with the essential abilities and information to arrive at informed conclusions about their monetary future.

3. **Correspondence and Family Gatherings:** Maintaining family unity and ensuring the smooth transfer of wealth necessitate honest and open communication among members of the family. Family values, objectives, and responsibilities can be discussed more easily at regular family gatherings. Additionally, these gatherings can be used to resolve potential disagreements, clarify expectations, and facilitate the exchange of plans and goals. Making a gathering for open discourse can assist with forestalling errors and advance solidarity among relatives.

4. **Proactive Initiative and Administration:** Allocating equipped and believed relatives as pioneers and chiefs in the family's abundance the board can decidedly affect generational abundance move. Laying out a family administration structure and carrying out strategies and systems can give a system to direction and resource the executives. Wealth is preserved and distributed in accordance with the family's vision and values thanks to this structure.

5. **Expand and Safeguard Resources**: A very much broadened venture portfolio can shield abundance from unexpected occasions and market instability. Spread speculations across various resource classes and

geological areas to diminish risk. Furthermore, consider the utilization of bequest arranging instruments, for example, trusts and establishments to shield resources from expected lenders, claims, and unnecessary tax assessment.

6. **Generosity and Social Obligation:** Integrating charity into your family's abundance move plan benefits society as well as imparts a feeling of direction and obligation inside people in the future. A great way to give back to the community and leave a positive legacy is to establish a family foundation or give to existing charitable organizations.

7. **Advice from a professional:** Looking for proficient exhortation from bequest organizers, monetary consultants, and abundance the executives specialists is critical in fostering a thorough generational abundance move plan. These professionals have the expertise and knowledge necessary to assist in the development of customized strategies that are compatible with the particular objectives and circumstances of your family. Investment management, tax-efficient estate planning, and the creation of trust structures are all areas in which they can be of assistance.

Guaranteeing generational abundance move and the making of an enduring heritage requires cautious preparation, proactive correspondence, and a pledge to monetary instruction. By beginning early, cultivating correspondence, enhancing resources, and looking for proficient direction, you can build the possibilities saving abundance and giving it to people in the future. In the end, leaving a legacy involves more than just money. It also includes family values, traditions, and chances for success in the future.

24 Offsetting accomplishment with satisfaction

In the present quick moving and hypercompetitive world, the quest for progress is frequently inseparable from the fulfillment of material abundance. Society puts extraordinary accentuation on the substantial markers of progress, like a lucrative work, sumptuous belongings, and cultural acknowledgment. Nonetheless, it is urgent to comprehend that genuine satisfaction and individual fulfillment go past these outer features.

Offsetting accomplishment with satisfaction includes discovering a more profound feeling of direction and significance in our lives. It necessitates investigating the mental, emotional, and spiritual facets of our being in addition to the material world. While material abundance is without a doubt significant for monetary security and an agreeable way of life, it alone can't ensure enduring joy.

We must shift our focus to cultivating relationships, pursuing our passions, and cultivating a sense of gratitude in order to find personal satisfaction beyond material wealth. Meaningful connections with loved ones frequently provide us with immense happiness and fulfillment. Constructing and keeping up with sound connections furnish us with the help, love, and understanding that material belongings can't offer. Embracing the associations that we have and putting time and exertion into keeping up with them can incredibly improve our general prosperity.

Besides, finding satisfaction includes recognizing and chasing after our interests, those exercises that touch off our excitement and present to us a feeling of direction. By participating in exercises that line up with our qualities, side interests, or interests, we experience a profound feeling of happiness as well as tap into our actual potential. These pursuits might be inventive undertakings like painting, composing, or playing music, or they might include committing investment to a reason or a local area project. Embracing our interests and pursuing accomplishing our objectives here can be enormously fulfilling and satisfying.

One more significant part of offsetting accomplishment with satisfaction is developing a feeling of appreciation. Appreciation permits us to see the value in the numerous endowments and delights that as of now exist in our lives. It moves our concentration from what we need or want to what we have and esteem. Finding opportunity to ponder the straightforward delights, important connections, and individual accomplishments in our lives can encourage satisfaction and a more profound feeling of satisfaction.

Giving back to others is another source of fulfillment and personal contentment. Thoughtful gestures, empathy, and administration bring a feeling of direction and satisfaction that outperforms any material riches. Offering our time, abilities, or assets to help those in need gives a significant feeling of satisfaction and adds to the long term benefit of society. Chipping in, coaching, and supporting worthy missions improve our lives as well as encourage a feeling of interconnectedness and have a constructive outcome on the planet.

Redefining what success means is essential if we are to strike a balance between happiness and success. We can take a more comprehensive approach that takes into account personal development, emotional well-being, and the contributions we make to society rather than focusing solely on external accomplishments and possessions as indicators of success. By moving our outlook towards finding individual fulfillment past material riches, we can make a satisfying and significant life that lines up with our qualities and desires.

In the end, conscious effort and self-reflection are necessary to strike a balance between fulfillment and success. It requires us to acknowledge our deepest desires, concentrate on the things that really matter, and align our actions with our values. We can create a life of fulfillment that goes far beyond material wealth by fostering relationships, pursuing our passions, cultivating gratitude, and giving back.

CONCLUSION

By embracing the tycoon outlook and carrying out the methodologies examined in this book, you will have the devices and information important to open the way to a nine-figure legacy. Achievement and abundance are inside your range, and with the right mentality, commitment, and assurance, you can make a phenomenal life for yourself, your friends, family, and leave an enduring effect on the world. The journey now begins!

www.ingramcontent.com/pod-product-compliance
Lightning Source LLC
Chambersburg PA
CBHW022345290526
45786CB00014B/2478